Come unto me, all ye that labour and are heavy laden, and I will give you rest. Take my yoke upon you, and learn of me; for I am meek and lowly in heart: and ye shall find rest unto your souls. For my yoke is easy, and my burden is light.

Jesus' words from the Gospel of Matthew

I tell you, do not worry about your life, what you will eat or drink; or about your body, what you will wear. Is not life more important than food, and the body more important than clothes? Look at the birds of the air; they do not sow or reap or store away in barns, and yet your heavenly Father feeds them. Are you not much more valuable than they?

Jesus' words from the Gospel of Matthew

Do not be anxious about anything, but in everything, by prayer and petition, with thanksgiving, present your requests to God. And the peace of God, which transcends all understanding, will guard your hearts and your minds in Christ Jesus.

From Paul's letter to the Philippians

Cast thy burden upon the Lord, and he shall sustain thee.

From Psalm 55

O give thanks to the Lord, for he is good,

for his steadfast love endures for ever;

to him who alone does great wonders,

for his steadfast love endures for ever;

to him who by understanding made the heavens,

for his steadfast love endures for ever;

to him who spread out the earth upon the waters,

for his steadfast love endures for ever;

to him who made the great lights,

for his steadfast love endures for ever;

the sun to rule over the day,

for his steadfast love endures for ever;

the moon and stars to rule over the night,

for his steadfast love endures for ever.

From Psalm 136

Peace I leave with you, my peace I give
unto you; not as the world giveth,
give I unto you. Let not your heart be
troubled, neither let it be afraid.

Jesus' words in the Gospel of John

God is our refuge and strength, an ever present help in trouble. Therefore we will not fear, though the earth give way and the mountains fall into the heart of the sea, though its waters roar and foam and the mountains quake with their surging.

From Psalm 46

Don't you know? Haven't you heard?
The Lord is the everlasting God;
   he created all the world.
He never grows tired or weary.
   No one understands his thoughts.
He strengthens those who are weak
   and tired.
Even those who are young grow weak;
   young people can fall exhausted.
But those who trust in the Lord for help
   will find their strength renewed.
They will rise on wings like eagles;
   they will run and not get weary;
   they will walk and not grow weak.

From the book of Isaiah

Trust in the Lord with all thine heart; and lean not unto thine own understanding. In all thy ways acknowledge him, and he shall direct thy paths.

From the book of Proverbs

There is a season for everything,

a time for every occupation under heaven. . .

a time for tears,

a time for laughter;

a time for mourning,

a time for dancing.

From Ecclesiastes 3

I sought the Lord, and he heard me,
and delivered me from my fears.

From Psalm 34

Be of good courage, and he shall strengthen
your heart, all ye that hope in the Lord.

From Psalm 31

I will never leave thee, nor forsake thee. So that we may boldly say, 'The Lord is my helper, and I will not fear what man shall do unto me.'

From the letter to the Hebrews

And why do you worry about clothes? See how the lilies of the field grow. They do not labour or spin. Yet I tell you that not even Solomon in all his splendour was dressed like one of these. If that is how God clothes the grass of the field, which is here today and tomorrow is thrown into the fire, will he not much more clothe you? . . . Do not worry about tomorrow, for tomorrow will worry about itself. Each day has enough trouble of its own.

Jesus' words from the Gospel of
Matthew

Come near to God and he will come near to you.

From the letter to James

Published by
Lion Publishing plc
Sandy Lane West, Oxford, England
ISBN 0 7459 3320 3
Albatross Books Pty Ltd
PO Box 320, Sutherland, NSW 2232, Australia
ISBN 0 7324 1268 4

First edition 1995
10 9 8 7 6 5 4 3 2 1 0

Picture acknowledgments
All photographs by Willi Rauch

Text acknowledgments
Scripture quotations are taken from the *Good News Bible* ©
American Bible Society, New York, 1966, 1971 and 4th
edition 1976, and published by Bible Societies/
HarperCollins; *The Holy Bible, New International Version*:
copyright © New York International Bible Society, 1973,
1978, 1984, and published by Hodder & Stoughton Ltd; the
Revised English Bible © 1970/1989 by permission of Oxford
and Cambridge University Presses; and the Authorized
Version of the Bible (the King James Bible), rights vested in
the Crown, and published by Cambridge University Press.

A catalogue record for this book is available
from the British Library

Printed and bound in Hong Kong